SOCIAL STUDIES EXPLORER

It's Cool to Learn About America's Waterways

THE EVERGLADES

➤ by Katie Marsico

Published in the United States of America
by Cherry Lake Publishing
Ann Arbor, Michigan
www.cherrylakepublishing.com

Content Adviser: James Wolfinger, PhD, Associate Professor,
History and Teacher Education, DePaul University, Chicago, Illinois

Book Design: The Design Lab

Photo Credits: Cover and page 3, ©Steve Byland/Shutterstock, Inc.,
©Anthony Ricci/Shutterstock, Inc., ©Audrey Snider-Bell/Shutterstock,
Inc., ©Holger W./Shutterstock, Inc., ©AlexanderZam/Shutterstock, Inc.;
back cover and page 3, ©FloridaStock/Shutterstock, Inc.; page 4, ©Jason
Patrick Ross/Shutterstock, Inc., page 7, ©Diane Uhley/Shutterstock, Inc.;
page 10, ©Matt Tilghman/Shutterstock, Inc.; page 11, ©J. Helgason/
Shutterstock, Inc.; page 12, ©jo Crebbin/Shutterstock, Inc., ©Rudy
Umans/Shutterstock, Inc.; page 16, ©Mary Evans Picture Library/
Alamy; page 18, ©Pictorial Press Ltd/Alamy; page 19, ©William Silver/
Shutterstock, Inc.; page 20, ©PHB.cz (Richard Semik)/Shutterstock, Inc.;
page 21, ©arnet117/Shutterstock, Inc.; page 24, ©Danita Delimont/
Alamy; page 25, ©FloridaStock/Shutterstock, Inc.; page 26, National Park
Service; page 27, USGS; page 29, ©Rudy Umans/Shutterstock, Inc.

Library of Congress Cataloging-in-Publication Data
Marsico, Katie, 1980–
    The Everglades / by Katie Marsico.
        p. cm. — (It's cool to learn about America's waterways)
    Includes bibliographical references and index.
    ISBN 978-1-62431-017-1 (lib. bdg.) — ISBN 978-1-62431-041-6 (pbk.)
— ISBN 978-1-62431-065-2 (e-book) 1. Everglades (Fla.)—Juvenile
literature. 2. Everglades National Park (Fla.)—Juvenile literature. I. Title.
    F317.E9M37 2013
    975.9'39—dc23   2012034738

Cherry Lake Publishing would like to acknowledge the work
of The Partnership for 21st Century Skills. Please visit
www.21stcenturyskills.org for more information.

Printed in the United States of America
Corporate Graphics Inc.
January 2013
CLSP12

THE EVERGLADES

TABLE OF CONTENTS

CHAPTER ONE
Welcome to the Everglades!...4

CHAPTER TWO
The Waterway's Wildlife...10

CHAPTER THREE
Past and Present...15

CHAPTER FOUR
**Taking Care of a
National Treasure...26**

Glossary.....................30
For More Information....31
Index.........................32
About the Author..........32

EVERGLADES
NATIONAL PARK
3¢

UNITED STATES POSTAGE

WELCOME TO THE EVERGLADES!

→ Alligators are one of the many types of animals that live in the Everglades.

Are you ready to tour the Everglades? The wetlands you are about to explore are filled with thousands of different plants and animals. Saw grass, **mangroves**, American alligators, and West Indian manatees are just a few examples of the wildlife you'll see! Many endangered species live in the Everglades. This wildlife is at risk of being lost forever. You'll learn about some of these plants and animals, as well as why this portion of Florida is extremely important to people. You'll uncover facts about everything from the Everglades' history to what local chefs are cooking up. (Get ready to sample frog legs!) As

you complete your journey, you'll find out what you can do to protect this amazing waterway.

The Everglades **ecosystem** is made up of about 2 million acres (809,371 hectares) of wetlands. It stretches from central Florida, near Orlando, to Florida Bay, which separates the mainland from the Florida Keys. Water from the Kissimmee River, which is located in the middle of the state, pours into shallow Lake Okeechobee in southeastern Florida. Overflow from the lake forms the Everglades, which is in fact a long, slow-moving river that winds 100 miles (161 kilometers) south toward Florida Bay. It measures about 50 miles (80 km) wide. Yet it is only a few feet deep in most spots.

A mixture of freshwater, **brackish** water, and seawater **habitats** are found in the Everglades. As a result, this wetland ecosystem is the only place on earth where alligators and crocodiles are found practically side by side. Most American alligators prefer freshwater environments. American crocodiles tend to seek out either brackish water or saltwater.

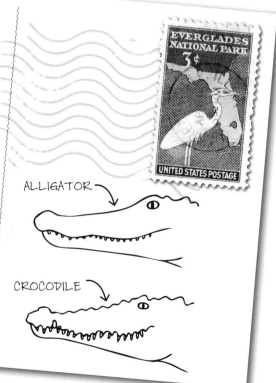

ALLIGATOR

CROCODILE

SOUTHERN FLORIDA MAP

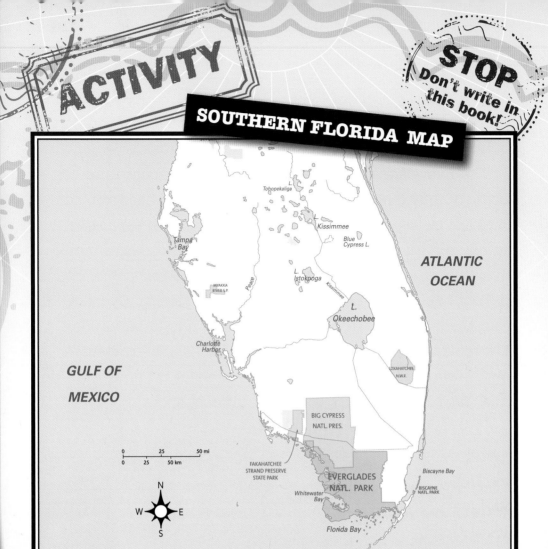

Tohopekaliga

L. Kissimmee

Blue Cypress L.

Tampa Bay

ATLANTIC OCEAN

MYAKKA RIVER S.P.

Peace

L. Istokpoga

Kissimmee

L. Okeechobee

Charlotte Harbor

GULF OF MEXICO

LOXAHATCHEE N.W.R.

BIG CYPRESS NATL. PRES.

0   25   50 mi
0   25   50 km

FAKAHATCHEE STRAND PRESERVE STATE PARK

Biscayne Bay

EVERGLADES NATL. PARK

BISCAYNE NATL. PARK

Whitewater Bay

N
W   E
S

Florida Bay

Straits of Florida

Take a close look at this map of Florida and the Everglades. Then place a separate piece of paper over it. Trace the outline of the wetland ecosystem. Use a crayon or marker to shade in the location of the Everglades. Next, label Lake Okeechobee, the Kissimmee River, Florida Bay, and other sites you have just learned about. As you continue reading, mark additional locations that you think are important to understanding this waterway.

➡ Thick green grass grows in many portions of the wetlands that make up the Everglades.

The Everglades is often called a "river of grass." This nickname refers to the endless blankets of saw grass that grow in the ecosystem's coastal marshes, swamps, and prairies. Pine forests and hardwood hammocks, which are thick clusters of broad-leaved trees, form part of the Everglades as well. So do mangroves located along the channels and rivers that flow near Florida's southern coast. Finally, Florida Bay adds approximately 800 square miles (2,072 sq km) of **marine** habitat to the Everglades.

You're probably eager to start exploring these different areas, but don't get ahead of yourself! First, you'll need to learn about the weather and climate. Then you can decide what clothes to pack.

The climate of the Everglades is semitropical. This means the region features humid, warm weather all year long. The average temperature in the Everglades ranges from 54 degrees Fahrenheit (12.2 degrees Celsius) to 95°F (35°C). Records show that it has gotten as cold as 24°F (−4.4°C) and as hot as 102°F (38.9°C). For the most part, however, temperatures rarely drop below freezing.

Hurricane season lasts from early June to late November. This is when powerful tropical storms sometimes whip along Florida's coastline. These storms bring destructive winds and heavy rainfall to the Everglades. Usually the rains are mild, however. Remember to tuck an umbrella somewhere in your suitcase!

You probably won't be doing a lot of swimming in the Everglades, but you should still know a little about the local water temperature. A recent study in the eastern Everglades showed that the water can get as hot as 97°F (36.1°C)! Even in winter, the water isn't usually much cooler than 59°F (15°C).

ACTIVITY

GRAPHING RAINFALL IN THE EVERGLADES

An average of 55 inches (1.4 meters) of rain falls in the Everglades each year. Rain that falls in winter (December through February) makes up about 9 percent of this amount. Rainfall in spring (March through May) represents 18 percent of the yearly total. Rain in summer (June through August) accounts for 44 percent of the annual amount. Finally, roughly 29 percent of their yearly rainfall comes in autumn (September through November).

Use this information to create a bar graph. Show how rainfall during each of the four seasons contributes to the total amount that soaks the Everglades over a period of 12 months. Which bar do you predict will be the longest? Which do you think will be the shortest?

STOP
Don't write in this book!

CHAPTER TWO

THE WATERWAY'S WILDLIFE

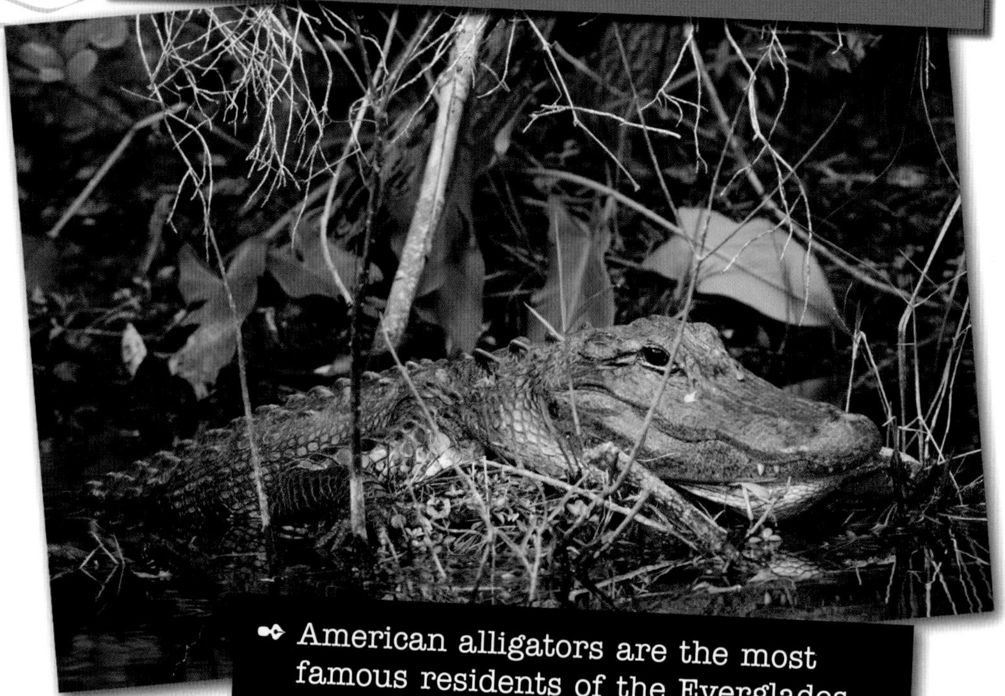

American alligators are the most famous residents of the Everglades.

Have you visited Florida before? If you answered yes, try to remember what you wore there. You probably spent most of your time in a swimsuit, shorts, and sandals. If you're touring the Everglades, however, you should rethink your outfit. You already know that you don't need to bring a winter jacket. Yet long pants, sleeved shirts, and closed shoes are a good idea if you plan to explore the wilderness.

Don't forget that one of the most common plants in the Everglades is saw grass—which has this name for a reason! Of course, the plant is not quite as sharp as an actual saw. Still, its blades have rough, spiky edges that can scratch your skin.

Think about packing a pair of binoculars if you hope to get a closer peek at other interesting plant life in the Everglades. They'll come in handy when it's time to study the cypress domes that dot the landscape. A cypress dome is a thick cypress swamp in which the trees grow close together. The tallest cypresses are usually found toward the center of the group. If you view a cypress dome from a distance, it almost seems as if you're staring at a rounded green roof.

◆➤ Cypress trees are a common sight in the Everglades.

◦→ The roseate spoonbill uses its spoon-shaped beak to scoop up small animals that live in the mud.

You probably already guessed that you should bring a camera on your tour of the Everglades. This way you can snap a few photos of mangroves, cabbage palms, slash pines, ferns, mosses, and **lichens**. Be sure to also get shots of any colorful orchids and **bromeliads** that catch your eye!

Keep in mind that you'll need to leave space on your camera for photographs of the hundreds of animals you will encounter. Approximately 350 kinds of birds, including snail kites, wood storks, and white and glossy ibises, are found in the Everglades. You may also glimpse roseate spoonbills, egrets, herons, and Cape Sable seaside sparrows, too.

These birds share their habitats with nearly 60 different types of reptiles. These include the alligators and crocodiles, the most famous creatures in the Everglades. The endangered Florida panther is among 76 species of mammals living in this ecosystem. Only between 100 and 160 Florida panthers exist in the world today! If you head closer to the coast, you may be lucky enough to photograph bottlenose dolphins. You might also spot another endangered mammal, the West Indian manatee. For now, however, pack your camera, zip up your suitcase, and prepare to do a little time traveling!

Keep your eyes peeled! The list of animals that live in the Everglades goes on and on. Scientists say 432 species of fish and 38 species of amphibians are found there. By the way, have you thought about throwing some bug spray in your suitcase? Thousands of different insects crawl, swim, and fly through Florida's southern wetlands!

Make Your Very Own Field Guide

Want to stay organized as you observe the countless plants and animals that live in the Everglades? Think about bringing a field guide. A field guide is a book that describes the different species found within a certain environment. If you follow the simple directions below, you won't need to buy a field guide before you head to the Everglades. You can create your own by selecting 20 local species (or more if you want). Write the name of each one on a separate sheet of paper. Next, get ready to do some detective work on the computer or at the library. Research and record the following information for the plants and animals you have chosen:

Type of plant/animal: (tree, shrub,
      flower/reptile, mammal, fish, etc.):
Habitat:
Appearance:
Other interesting facts:

When you're done, either print out or sketch pictures of the species in your guidebook. Finally, decorate a cover and staple your pages together. You could also snap them into a binder. Don't forget to pack your field guide before you begin your journey through the Everglades!

CHAPTER THREE

PAST AND PRESENT

➾ The Everglades once stretched across even more land in southern Florida.

Close your eyes and pretend that you're not touring the Everglades during the 21st century. Instead, imagine that you've gone back in time about 5,000 years! Scientists believe that this is when climate changes led to the formation of Florida's famous wetland ecosystem. You'll have to use your imagination because the Everglades region then was much different than it is now.

At that time, the Everglades made up a far larger portion of southern Florida. Even centuries later—in the early 1900s— the wetlands stretched over 11,000 square miles (28,490 sq km). That's almost twice what the Everglades measured in 2012! Human activity gradually shrunk the wetlands to their current size.

People have been present in the Everglades for thousands of years. Calusa, Tequesta, Jeaga, and Ais Indians fished there. The Calusa used seashells to build mounds, courtyards, and platforms in their villages. Spanish explorers arrived in southern Florida starting in the early 1500s. The Europeans forced many American Indians into slavery and introduced diseases that killed off countless others. Several native groups began to disappear from the area.

Some 16th-century Europeans who traveled through the Everglades were hunting for gold, treasure, and slaves. Spanish explorer Juan Ponce de León, however, was also searching for something else—eternal youth! In 1513, he arrived in Florida with the hope of locating a magical fountain. He believed its waters had the power to keep people young forever. Ponce de León never found the fountain of youth, but there is a bay named after him in the Everglades.

ACTIVITY

TEST YOUR KNOWLEDGE

How much do you know about the history of the Everglades? Find out by taking the matching quiz below! On the left side of this activity, you will see the names of five people who are linked to the Everglades. On the right side, you will see the reasons these men and women are famous. Try to match each person with the correct description!

1) Juan Ponce de León

A) Wife of a former Florida governor and famous supporter of environmental protection and women's voting rights; she helped develop Royal Palm State Park (which later became part of Everglades National Park)

2) Osceola

B) Florida politician who became well-known for his efforts to build canals throughout the Everglades and drain local wetlands

3) Napoleon Bonaparte Broward

C) Spanish explorer who discovered Florida and the Everglades while searching for a magical fountain that supposedly helped people stay young forever

4) May Mann Jennings

D) American author who first described the Everglades as a "river of grass" and who dedicated much of her life to protecting it and other natural areas

5) Marjory Stoneman Douglas

E) American Indian leader who led his people against U.S. troops during the Seminole Wars

Answers: 1) C; 2) E; 3) B; 4) A; 5) D

STOP
Don't write in this book!

In the 1700s, Seminole Indians began living in the Everglades. Between 1818 and 1858, they fought the U.S. government in a series of three armed conflicts that became known as the Seminole Wars. The government wanted to seize American Indian lands for white settlers and move the Seminoles west of the Mississippi River. After years of bloodshed, the Seminole population was drastically reduced and most of the remaining Seminoles reluctantly left their Florida homelands. Ultimately, however, they had a major influence on local culture that continues to shape the Everglades today.

During the next few centuries, various European nations claimed control of parts of present-day Florida that included the Everglades. Then, in 1821, Florida became a U.S. territory. It gained statehood in 1845. At first, some Americans saw the Everglades as little more than a wild swamp crawling with snakes and alligators. Eventually, however, the rich wildlife there attracted growing numbers of fishers and hunters.

Settlers began establishing farms and communities within the Everglades. They constructed canals to control and redirect the flow of water. By the late 1920s, railroad tracks and the Tamiami Trail—a highway linking Florida's east and west coasts—zigzagged through the area. Today, five Florida counties cover parts of the Everglades. They are Monroe, Collier, Palm Beach, Miami-Dade, and Broward.

The Tamiami Trail, which cuts through the Everglades, is an important transportation route in Florida.

●→ Everglades National Park is a popular tourist destination.

Southern Florida continued to grow and change. Some people began to worry about the effect that human activity was having on plants and animals in the Everglades. In 1947, Americans concerned about the future of these wetlands established Everglades National Park. About 75 percent of the Everglades lies within its boundaries. Hunting is not allowed there, and the land is free from further development. You will take a closer look at other **conservation** efforts toward the end of your Everglades adventure. For the moment, however, wrap up your travels through time. Prepare to set foot inside Everglades National Park!

What do you want to do first? Hiking, kayaking, canoeing, biking, bird-watching, fishing, and camping are all popular activities. Many people also take guided tours of the park.

Some tours are given in swamp buggies or airboats. A swamp buggy is a type of vehicle that can move both on land and in water. An airboat is a lightweight, flat-bottomed boat. It is driven by a propeller that spins in the air.

Don't forget to take a breather between tours and grab a bite to eat. Many restaurants offer fresh seafood such as oysters, lobster, and stone crab. Of course, you could be truly adventurous and sample fried frog legs and alligator nuggets! This second dish is made from alligator meat. The meat is cut into cubes and cooked in batter. (Don't be nervous about digging in—a lot of people say alligator nuggets taste a little like chewy chicken.) Other popular menu items in the Everglades include catfish, Indian fry bread, and pumpkin bread.

Huge propellers push airboats through the waters of the Everglades.

Indian fry bread is a favorite addition to many meals in the Everglades. This Seminole flat dough can be served either alone or as a kind of shell that can be stuffed with everything from fruit to taco fillings. You can make your own batch of Indian fry bread at home. Just be sure to have an adult help you use the stove and handle the hot cooking oil!

Indian Fry Bread

INGREDIENTS
4 cups flour
1 tablespoon sugar
2 teaspoons salt
1 tablespoon baking powder
1 tablespoon shortening
2 cups milk or water
2 cups cooking oil

INSTRUCTIONS

1. Mix the flour, sugar, salt, and baking powder together in a bowl. Stir in the shortening and milk (or water, depending on your preference).

2. Use your hands to work the mixture into a soft dough.

3. Sprinkle a few pinches of flour on the surface of a baking sheet. Roll the dough onto this sheet and flatten it with your hands or a rolling pin.

4. Use either your fingers or a plastic knife to break the dough into six to eight small squares measuring about ½ inch (1.3 centimeters) thick.

5. Pour the cooking oil into a saucepan. Warm it over medium heat on your stovetop.

6. Carefully drop each of the squares (one at a time) into the hot oil. Keep a close eye on them! In about 2 to 4 minutes, they should rise to the surface of the oil and turn brownish-gold in color. Use a long spoon or spatula to flip the squares over. Continue frying them for a few more minutes.

7. Turn off the stove and remove the squares from the oil with a slotted spoon. Place your Indian fry bread on a paper towel and let any extra oil drain from the individual pieces before serving.

◆ Many people who work in the Everglades have jobs related to tourism.

Would you be surprised to discover that your journey has an impact on the **economy** of the Everglades? Tourism and **recreational** activities are important businesses in this part of Florida. So are real estate and fishing. In addition, farmers grow crops such as sugarcane, sod, rice, beans, lettuce, and celery in the Everglades.

Residents depend on this ecosystem in other ways as well. About one in three Floridians rely on the Everglades as a source of freshwater. The trees that grow there even act as natural filters. Their roots absorb, or take in, different minerals and chemicals that make the water impure, or unclean.

The Everglades also serve as a buffer, or block. They prevent nearby areas from flooding. The plant life, sand, soil, and land formations there help soak up extra water that might otherwise cause damage to towns and cities throughout southern Florida.

Scientists and conservationists continue to study the Everglades to learn more about the plants and animals that live within this ecosystem. Sadly, human activity has already had a destructive effect on many species and their habitats.

◦◦ Scientists use water meters to measure how much rain falls in different parts of the Everglades.

CHAPTER FOUR

TAKING CARE OF A NATIONAL TREASURE

➥ Volunteers of all ages perform conservation work in the Everglades.

You're coming to the end of your Everglades adventure. But that doesn't mean you can kick back and relax! It is up to Americans of all ages to do their part to protect southern Florida's delicate wetlands. Luckily, more people are beginning to understand that the Everglades may continue to disappear.

Remember that the size of this ecosystem has shrunk over time. The construction of canals, dams, buildings, and farms has

resulted in water being drained, redirected, and polluted. Loss of habitat and overhunting have taken a serious toll on wildlife. Scientists currently list 67 species that live in the Everglades as being either endangered or threatened. Endangered species have a high risk of being completely wiped out. Threatened species are those that face becoming endangered.

The destruction of the Everglades is also bad for the human residents of Florida. The wetlands affect everything from the state's economy to flood control to the availability of drinking water. They also provide people all over the world with the opportunity to explore a unique American ecosystem.

Not all of the wildlife found in the Everglades belongs there! Burmese pythons, Cuban tree frogs, wild boars, and Japanese climbing fern are examples of **invasive** species. The Everglades is not part of their native environment. People have either purposely or accidentally introduced these plants and animals into the Everglades. Invasive species tend to reproduce quickly within a new habitat. They frequently spread diseases, eat native wildlife, and compete with native plants and animals for food, water, and living space.

Political leaders from Florida to Washington, D.C., and beyond have the power to shape the future of the Everglades. These men and women make important decisions about laws and government projects that protect America's waterways. Writing a letter to such individuals makes them aware that you care about Florida's wetlands. Ask an adult to help you find the addresses of politicians involved with conservation of the Everglades. Then create a short, simple letter using the following outline:

Dear [INSERT THE NAME OF THE POLITICIAN(S) YOU DECIDE TO WRITE TO]:

I am writing to ask for your help in protecting the Everglades. These wetlands are important to me because [INSERT TWO OR THREE REASONS THE EVERGLADES MATTER TO YOU].

Thanks for your efforts to support this amazing American waterway!

Sincerely,

[INSERT YOUR NAME]

Everyone is responsible for the future of the Everglades. Fortunately, many scientists, government leaders, and everyday citizens like you are working together to support conservation. Their efforts include treating polluted water so that it is clean by the time it flows into the Everglades. Other Americans are studying ways to reverse the damaging effects of canals and other projects.

How can you help? For starters, you can share all that you've learned during your Everglades adventure! Let your friends, family, and community know why this American waterway is so remarkable—and why it deserves respect and protection.

➥ Think about some other ways you can help preserve the natural beauty of the Everglades.

GLOSSARY

brackish (BRAK-ish) water that is saltier than freshwater but not as salty as seawater

bromeliads (bro-MEE-lee-adz) plants with short stems and rose-shaped clusters of stiff, spiny leaves

conservation (kahn-sur-VAY-shuhn) the protection of valuable things, especially wildlife, natural resources, forests, or artistic or historic objects

economy (i-KAH-nuh-mee) the system of buying, selling, making things, and managing money in a place

ecosystem (EE-koh-sis-tuhm) all the livings things in a place and their relation to the environment

habitats (HAB-uh-tats) places where an animal or a plant naturally lives

invasive (in-VAY-siv) tending to spread through and dominate a region to which a thing is not native, such as plants and animals that have been brought into a region

lichens (LYE-kuhnz) flat, spongy growths on rocks, walls, and trees that consist of algae and fungi growing close together

mangroves (MAN-grohvz) trees or shrubs that grow in saltwater and have roots that rise into the air

marine (muh-REEN) of or having to do with the ocean

recreational (rek-ree-AY-shuhn-uhl) involving games, sports, and hobbies that people like to do in their spare time

FOR MORE INFORMATION

BOOKS

Corwin, Jeff. *The Extraordinary Everglades*. New York: Grosset & Dunlap, 2010.

Larsen, Laurel, and Joyce Mihran Turley (illustrator). *One Night in the Everglades*. Lanham, MD: Taylor Trade Publishing, 2012.

WEB SITES

Friends of the Everglades—Young Friends
www.everglades.org/young-friends
This Web site features videos, fast facts, and information about what young Americans are doing to protect the Everglades.

The National Park Service—Everglades National Park for Kids
www.nps.gov/ever/forkids/index.htm
Check out additional information about the Everglades and how you can become a junior park ranger there.

airboats, 21
alligators, 4, 5, 10, 13, 18, 21
amphibian life, 13, 21, 27
animal life, 4, 12, 14, 20, 25, 27

birds, 12, 20
bottlenose dolphins, 13
brackish water, 5
bromeliads, 12
Broward County, 19
Broward, Napoleon Bonaparte, 17

canals, 17, 19, 26–27, 29
climate, 7, 8, 15
Collier County, 19
conservation, 20, 25, 26, 28, 29
crocodiles, 5, 13
cypress domes, 11

dams, 26–27
depth, 5
diseases, 16, 27
Douglas, Marjory Stoneman, 17
drinking water, 27

economy, 24, 27
ecosystems, 5, 6, 7, 13, 15, 24, 25, 26–27
endangered species, 4, 13, 27
European exploration, 16, 17, 18
Everglades National Park, 17, 20

farming, 19, 24, 26–27
field guides, 14
fishing, 16, 18, 20, 24
flooding, 25, 27
Florida Bay, 5, 6, 7
Florida Keys, 5
foods, 21, 22–23
freshwater, 5, 24, 27, 29

habitats, 7, 13, 25, 27
hunting, 18, 20, 27
hurricanes, 8

Indian Fry Bread, 21, 22–23
insect life, 13

invasive species, 27

Jennings, May Mann, 17

Kissimmee River, 5, 6

Lake Okeechobee, 5, 6
land area, 5, 7, 15–16
laws, 28
lichens, 12

mangroves, 4, 7, 12
map, 6
marine life, 7, 13, 16, 20, 21
Miami-Dade County, 19
Monroe County, 19

Native Americans, 16, 17, 18, 22

Osceola (Seminole leader), 17

Palm Beach County, 19
plant life, 4, 7, 11–12, 14, 20, 24, 25, 27
politicians, 17, 28, 29
pollution, 27, 29
Ponce de León, Juan, 16, 17

railroads, 19
rainfall, 8, 9
recipe, 22–23
reptilian life, 5, 13, 18, 21, 27
roadways, 19
roseate spoonbills, 12

saw grass, 7, 11
seawater, 5
Seminole Wars, 17, 18
settlers, 18–19
size, 5, 7, 16, 26–27
swamp buggies, 21

Tamiami Trail, 19
temperatures, 8
threatened species, 27
tourism, 20–21, 24
trees, 7, 11, 24

water temperatures, 8
weather, 8, 9
West Indian manatees, 13
width, 5

ABOUT THE AUTHOR
Katie Marsico has written more than 100 books for young readers. She hopes to tour the Everglades during her next visit to Florida.